LEARNING HOW WORDS WORK

Written by Trisha Callella

Editor: Kim Cernek

Illustrator: John Jones

Cover Illustrator: Kimberly Schamber

Designer: Jane Wong Saunders

Cover Designer: Moonhee Pak

Art Director: Tom Cochrane

Project Director: Carolea Williams

Table of Contents

Over 500 common primary words can be spelled with only 37 phonograms, or "packages" of sounds. Commonly referred to as "word families," we combine sounds with consonants, blends, and digraphs to make words. Students who easily recognize the spelling patterns of these familiar phonograms learn to read and write more effectively.

Fun with Phonograms helps you teach students "how words work." Once students can identify common word parts, they will be able to generalize this information to create a greater number of words. Use the program outlined in this book to give your beginning readers many opportunities to hear and generate rhymes. Once students are able to auditorily identify and produce rhyming sounds, they will be ready to read and write them. Adapt the activity ideas in this book for use with any phonogram. Use the reproducible phonogram cards and phonogram word lists to minimize planning and preparation time.

Each of the 37 phonograms that appear in almost every word primary students will encounter as they learn to read is featured in *Fun with Phonograms*. Each phonogram is highlighted in an original poem or story that students can read aloud with the class or on their own. A puzzle that features additional words with the phonogram follows each poem or story to provide students with extra practice and review.

This fun and easy approach to teaching students how to identify and produce words using 37 common phonograms fits easily into your daily classroom routine and will strengthen your language arts program!

Getting Started

The phonograms in this book are arranged in alphabetical order, but you can customize your own program. Focus on phonograms with silent e (e.g., *-ake, -ice, -ide*) or short vowel sounds (e.g., *-at, -est, -ock*) over the course of several weeks. Or, choose a poem or story that fits your current theme, and have students explore the phonogram highlighted in it (e.g., *-ine* words for Valentine's Day).

Activities

Use one or two activities (see pages 6–10) to introduce a new phonogram at the beginning of each week. Use the reproducible phonogram cards (pages 11–16) and phonogram word lists (pages 17–22) with these activities or ones you create on your own. At the end of the week, have students use the phonogram to read the poem or story and complete the coordinating puzzle activity.

Stories

Photocopy a story on an overhead transparency, and display it. Invite students to help you read it aloud. Have students identify words that contain the phonogram, and circle them with a dry erase marker. Or, copy the story, use correction fluid to delete the word family words, and photocopy the page on an overhead transparency. Use a dry erase marker to write the words you deleted at the bottom of the page, and have students read them aloud. Then, expose only one sentence at a time, and ask students to fill in each blank. For extra practice, give students a copy of the story to read on their own in class or at home. Have students circle the words that contain the current phonogram and previous ones. Also, challenge students to look for the phonogram within words (e.g., *-ick* in *chicken*).

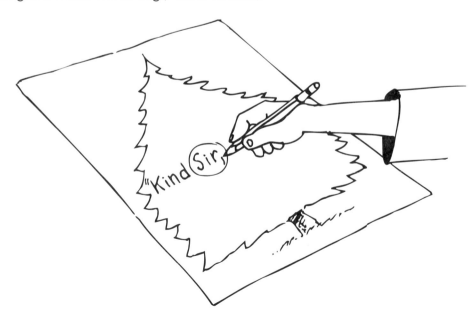

Poems

You can use the poems the same way you use the stories or write the words on separate sentence strips, and have students help you supply the missing words. Place the strips in order in a pocket chart, and invite the class to read the poem aloud. Then, invite students to point to the words that contain the "phonogram-of-the-week." Encourage students to also identify words with phonograms from past weeks.

Puzzles

Each story or poem is followed by ten sentences and a list of words with the coordinating phonogram. Have students work independently or with a partner to read the words at the top of the page and then use each one to complete a sentence. Tell students to write each word in the boxes at the end of the sentence. Explain that only one letter fits in each box. Tell students that the missing word for a sentence with a star features the phonogram within the word. Review the completed sentences together as a class.

Name _____   Date _____

-ink

think	sink	blink
link	pink	stink
rink	wink	drink
		mink

1. Do you like the color _____?

2. Please wash the dishes in the _____.

3. Do you _____ your eyes when it is windy?

4. I went to the skating _____.

5. Did you just _____ your eye at me?

6. What is that smell? Does it _____!

7. What do you _____ will happen in the next chapter of our book?

8. I could use a _____ of lemonade on this hot day!

9. She does not have a _____ coat.

10. Let's _____ arms and skate together.

74

Fun with Phonograms © 2300 Creative Teaching Press

Activities

Materials

–Phonogram Cards
 (pages 11–16)

–scissors

–tape

–index cards

Word Families Word Wall

Identify an area of wall space in your classroom where you can display words that contain each phonogram. Introduce a new phonogram (e.g., -ip), copy and cut out its phonogram card, and tape it to the wall. Encourage students to think of words in this word family (e.g., hip, lip, zip). Write each word on a separate index card, and tape the cards below the phonogram. Repeat this process each week with a new phonogram. Encourage students to refer to the word wall to help them read and spell word family words.

_ing	_ock	_ug
king	block	bug
ring	clock	hug
sing	rock	rug

Materials

–sentence strip
 halves

Alphabetical Order

Choose a phonogram, and invite students to brainstorm words that feature it. Write each word on a separate sentence strip half, and give each strip to a student. Slowly say aloud the alphabet, and invite the students who are holding a word card that begins with each letter to stand in a line. Invite those students who are not holding a word card to read aloud the words in the order they appear after all of the letters of the alphabet have been called. Collect the word cards, pass them out to different students, and repeat the activity.

Phonogram Cards

This activity is perfect for a learning center. Copy one page of phonogram cards, and cut them apart. Tape a phonogram card (e.g., *-ight*) to a cookie sheet or magnetic board, and place magnetic letters below it. Invite students to place letters in front of the phonogram to create real words (e.g., *light, bright*) and then write them on a piece of paper. Encourage students to repeat the activity with a new phonogram or add letters to the end of the phonogram to create new words (e.g., *lighter, brighten*).

Materials
-Phonogram Cards
 (pages 11-16)
-scissors
-tape
-cookie sheet or
 magnetic board
-magnetic letters
-writing paper

Word Family Sorting

Write the same number of words from two different word families on separate sentence strip halves, and place them in a large envelope. Invite a small group of students to sort the cards into the two piles. Encourage students to record the words for each family on separate pieces of writing paper. To extend learning, add a third set of word family cards to the envelope.

Materials
-sentence strip
 halves
-large envelope
-writing paper

Materials

–index cards
–pocket chart
–chart paper

Secret Word Game

Choose a content area vocabulary word or one from your literature unit that features the phonogram-of-the-week (e.g., *continents* for the phonogram *-in*). Write each letter of the word on a separate index card. Place the cards in random order in a pocket chart. Invite students to rearrange the letters to make as many words as they can, and write them on a piece of chart paper next to the pocket chart. Challenge students to assemble the letters in order to spell the secret word. Remind students to use the phonogram-of-the-week to help them spell the word.

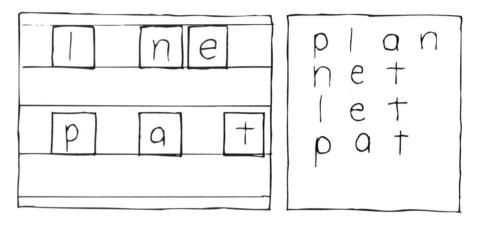

Materials

–dry erase board
 (optional)

Words within Words

Each day choose a multisyllabic word that features the phonogram-of-the-week (e.g., *daily* for *-ail* or *handle* for *-and*), and write it on a chalkboard or dry erase board. Teach students to mentally break the word into "chunks" of sound (e.g., daily is /d/ /ail/ /y/). Invite students to circle the phonogram-of-the-week in the word. Have students blend the sounds together to read the new word.

Morning Message and Daily News

Include words that feature the phonogram-of-the-week in your class's morning message or daily news report. For example, write the following message on a chalkboard or dry erase board for students to read and/or copy on writing paper during the week that you introduce -*ight*:

Today is Monday, September 21. Tonight is Family Night at school. We will show our families how bright we are!

Invite students to circle the words in the message that feature the phonogram-of-the-week.

Materials

–dry erase board and writing paper (optional)

Can You Guess My Word?

Cut a large piece of construction paper in half horizontally. Staple the two long sides of one half to a bulletin board to create a sleeve. Slightly trim the other half of paper, write a word with the phonogram-of-the-week (e.g., *shocking*) on it, and slip it in the paper sleeve. Pull out the paper to expose the first letter or letters that make the first sound of the word (i.e., *sh*). Invite the class to say the sound aloud. Pull out the paper to expose the letter or letters for the next sound in the word (i.e., *ock*), and have the class say the new sound. Encourage the class to blend the first sound with the second sound. Repeat the process with the next sound or sounds until students have read the complete word. Remind students that they can read any word by breaking it down into smaller parts.

Materials

–scissors
–construction paper
–stapler

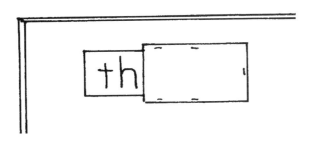

Materials

-Phonogram Cards
 (pages 11-16)
-magnetic letters
 or letter cards
-writing paper

Word Wizards

Invite students to work in groups of three or four. Choose one page of phonogram cards, and make a copy for each student. Give each student a magnetic letter or letter card. Ask students to place their letter before each rime on their paper. Have students write the real words they make on a piece of paper. After a few minutes, tell the students to pass their letter to the person sitting to their right and repeat the process. Continue until each student has manipulated every letter in the group. Invite students to compare their lists. Give each student a copy of a different page of phonogram cards and a new magnetic letter or card, and repeat the activity.

Materials

-phonogram puzzles
-writing paper
-crayons or
 markers

Puzzle Extensions

After students complete the puzzle page that appears after each story or poem, invite them to use the words in the word bank or add a prefix or suffix to these words to write new sentence puzzles. Or, have students choose a few words from the word bank, use them to write a sentence or two, and illustrate their sentence or sentences.

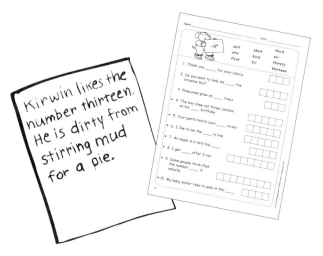

_ack	_ail
_ain	_ake
_ale	_ame

Fun with Phonograms © 2000 Creative Teaching Press

_an	_ank
_ap	_ash
_at	_ate

Fun with Phonograms © 2000 Creative Teaching Press

_aw	
_ay	_eat
_ell	_est
_ice	_ick

_ide	_ight
_ill	_in
_ine	_ing

14

_ink	_ip
_ir	_ock
_oke	_op

_or	_ore
_uck	_ug
_ump	_unk

Fun with Phonograms © 2000 Creative Teaching Press

back	pack	smack
backpack	quack	snack
black	rack	stack
crack	sack	tack
haystack	shack	track
jack	slacks	whack
knack		
lack		

-ack

bail	mail	sail
detail	nail	snail
fail	pail	tail
frail	quail	toenail
hail	rail	trail
jail		

-ail

brain	grain	sprain
chain	main	stain
complain	pain	strain
contain	rain	train
drain	refrain	vain
explain	remain	
gain		

-ain

awake	lake	sake
bake	make	shake
brake	mistake	snake
cake	pancake	snowflake
cupcake	quake	stake
fake	rake	take
flake		

-ake

exhale	male	stale
female	pale	tale
gale	sale	whale
inhale	scale	

-ale

became	frame	nickname
blame	game	same
came	lame	shame
fame	name	tame
flame		

-ame

-an

an	man	span
ban	pan	suntan
began	pancake	tan
bran	plan	than
can	ran	trashcan
clan	scan	van
fan		

-ank

bank	prank	stank
blank	rank	tank
clank	sank	thank
crank	shrank	yank
drank	spank	
frank		
plank		

-ap

cap	nap	strap
chap	rap	tap
clap	sap	trap
flap	scrap	wrap
gap	slap	yap
lap	snap	zap
map		

-ash

ash	gash	slash
bash	hash	smash
cash	lash	splash
clash	mash	stash
crash	rash	thrash
dash	sash	trash
flash		

-at

at	flat	sat
bat	habitat	scat
brat	hat	splat
cat	mat	that
chat	pat	vat
fat	rat	

-ate

ate	fate	migrate
celebrate	gate	plate
crate	grate	rate
create	hate	relate
date	late	rotate
decorate	locate	skate
donate	mate	state
educate		
estate		
estimate		

-aw

caw	law	straw
claw	paw	thaw
draw	raw	
flaw	saw	
gnaw		
jaw		

-ay

away	hooray	stay
bay	lay	stray
clay	may	sway
day	okay	today
decay	pay	tray
display	play	way
gray	pray	weekday
halfway	ray	yesterday
hallway	relay	
hay	say	
highway	slay	
holiday	spray	

-eat

backseat	feat	seat
beat	heat	treat
bleat	meat	wheat
cheat	neat	
defeat		
eat		

-ell

bell	jell	spell
cell	retell	swell
dell	sell	tell
dwell	shell	well
fell	smell	yell

-est

best	nest	test
chest	pest	vest
crest	protest	west
detest	quest	zest
guest	rest	
invest	suggest	
jest		

-ice

advice	nice	spice
device	price	twice
dice	rice	vice
ice	slice	
lice		
mice		

brick	pick	thick
candlestick	prick	tick
chick	quick	toothpick
chopstick	seasick	trick
click	sick	wick
flick	slick	yardstick
kick	stick	
lick		
nick		

-ick

beside	hide	side
bride	inside	slide
collide	outside	stride
decide	pride	tide
divide	ride	wide
glide		
guide		

-ide

bright	knight	sight
daylight	light	slight
delight	might	sunlight
fight	night	tight
flashlight	right	tonight
flight		
fright		
height		

-ight

bill	hill	skill
chill	ill	spill
dill	kill	thrill
drill	mill	will
fill	pill	
frill	sill	
gill		
grill		

-ill

begin	pin	tin
bin	shin	twin
chin	sin	violin
din	skin	win
fin	spin	within
grin	thin	
in		
kin		

-in

canine	nine	swine
combine	outline	twine
deadline	pine	vine
dine	shine	whine
divine	spine	wine
feline	sunshine	
fine		
line		
mine		

-ine

Fun with Phonograms © 2000 Creative Teaching Press

anything	sing	swing
bring	sling	thing
cling	something	wing
ding	spring	wring
everything	sting	zing
fling	string	
king		
ping		**-ing**
ring		

blink	rink	stink
clink	shrink	think
drink	sink	wink
ink	slink	
link		
mink		
pink		**-ink**

chip	nip	spaceship
clip	rip	strip
dip	ship	tip
drip	sip	trip
flip	skip	whip
grip	slip	zip
hip	snip	
lip		**-ip**

fir	sir	stir

-ir

artichoke	smoke	stroke
broke	spoke	woke
choke		
joke		**-oke**
poke		

block	lock	socks
clock	mock	stock
dock	rock	tock
flock	shock	unlock
frock	smock	
jock		
knock		**-ock**

bop	lollipop	shop
chop	mop	slop
clop	nonstop	stop
cop	plop	top
crop	pop	workshop
drop	prop	
flop	raindrop	
hop		**-op**

condor	nor	senior
for	or	señor
matador		

-or

adore	more	sore
before	pore	store
bore	score	swore
chore	seashore	tore
core	shore	wore
encore	snore	
ignore		

-ore

buck	muck	truck
chuck	pluck	tuck
cluck	puck	yuck
duck	struck	
luck	suck	

-uck

bug	plug	snug
drug	rug	thug
dug	shrug	tug
hug	slug	
jug	smug	
lug		
mug		

-ug

bump	plump	stump
chump	pump	thump
clump	rump	trump
dump	slump	
jump		
lump		

-ump

bunk	junk	stunk
chunk	shrunk	sunk
drunk	skunk	trunk
dunk	spunk	
flunk		
funk		
hunk		

-unk

Fun with Phonograms © 2000 Creative Teaching Press

Jack's Wacky Day

Jack woke up and couldn't believe his eyes. He went to pack for a trip to his grandma's house, but his black shirt and slacks were missing. He checked the rack in his closet, but they weren't there. Then he went to look for a stack of books he wanted to read on the trip, but they were gone, too! He closed his eyes. Then he opened them just a crack to see if he was just dreaming. He sat down and ate some crackers for a snack. He thought, "What a wacky day!" I think I'll just go back to bed.

Can you find 11 different words with –ack?

pack	crack	crackers
snack	sack	back
slacks	black	stack
		rack

1. I will _____ my bag for my trip.

2. Don't drop the egg or it will _____.

3. My favorite colors are red and _____.

4. Will you please scratch my _____?

5. I put my lunch in a paper _____.

6. I have a big _____ of books.

7. I will eat a _____ after school.

8. Hang your clothes on that _____.

＊ 9. Would you like some
    cheese and _____?

＊10. I put on my shirt and _____.

Fun with Phonograms © 2000 Creative Teaching Press

The Sailor

Early one morning, a sailor woke up and noticed that it was raining hard. The rain froze and turned to hail, so he decided to sail his boat back to land. When he got there, he used one hand to carry his pail of fish and the other hand to hold the rail as he walked off the boat. He was hungry, so he ate breakfast at the same restaurant he ate at daily. After breakfast, he went to the post office to pick up his mail. He stopped along the way to pet a dog that was wagging its tail. Together, they waited for the rain to stop.

Can you find 8 different words with *-ail*?

Name _____   Date_____

sail	fail	rail
hail	jail	sailor
tail	nail	mail
		pail

1. Try hard, and you will not _____.

2. I put some water in the _____.

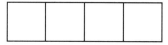

3. I got a letter in the _____.

4. The robber had to go to _____.

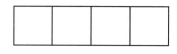

5. Use a hammer and a _____ to hang that picture.

6. I love to _____ on the ocean.

7. I hold the _____ when I walk up the stairs.

8. Rain that freezes is called _____.

9. A monkey can hang from its _____.

* 10. The _____ went to sea.

The Stain

I can't explain
This bright red stain
I see on my big toe.

I've searched my brain.
(And now it's in pain!)
But still I just don't know.

I could complain,
But I will refrain
And leave my toe just so.

Can you find 6 different words with *-ain*?

Name _____ Date _____

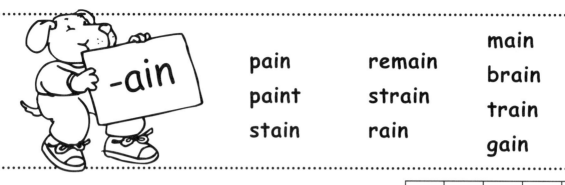

pain   remain   main
paint   strain   brain
stain   rain   train
                  gain

1. That ink might _____ your shirt.

2. The _____ will help our flowers grow.

3. I think with my _____.

4. I fell on my knees, and now I am in _____.

5. Try not to _____ your back.

6. When you are in trouble, _____ calm.

7. What is the _____ idea of your story?

8. You need to _____ some weight.

9. Look for a _____ before you cross the tracks.

* 10. She has green _____ on her bedroom walls.

Fun with Phonograms © 2000 Creative Teaching Press

A Whale of a Tale

Dale and Carlos loved the sea. They loved to swim and go fishing. One day, they saw a boat for sale, so they bought it. It was a pale yellow color. The next day, they invited their friends, Megan and Haley, to go for a boat ride. They waited for a big gale of wind to push them out to sea. There they caught three big fish. Haley weighed them on a scale. Dale said that once he caught a fish that was as big as a whale. Of course, he was just telling a tale. They ate the fish for dinner and planned another boat trip for next week.

Can you find 8 different words with –ale?

Name _____ Date _____

-ale

inhale	stale	whale
bale	sale	tale
scale	male	pale
		exhale

1. A ____ breathes through its blowhole.

2. Old bread tastes ____.

3. My face looks ____ when I am sick.

4. This cat is a boy, so it is a ____.

5. I sat on a ____ of hay at the farm.

6. There is a big ____ at the toy store today.

7. Your story sounds like a fairy ____.

8. When you breathe in, you ____.

9. When you breath out, you ____.

10. Let's weigh the fruit on a ____.

Fun with Phonograms © 2000 Creative Teaching Press

The Name Game

Let's play a name game.

I'll say a word, and you say a name.

Remember, when you play this game,

Both of our words must sound the same.

If I say *cake,* then you say *Jake.*

If I say *plan,* then you say *Stan.*

It doesn't matter whose name you say,

As long as it rhymes in some way.

(Use the names of children in your class to continue the game.)

Can you find 3 different words with –ame?

lame   blame   came

name   became   same

game   frame   flame

    tame

1. What is your ____?

2. A wild animal is not ____.

3. Will you play a ____ with me?

4. There is a picture of my grandmother in that ____.

5. I ____ to school early today.

6. I don't ____ others for my mistakes.

7. The candle has a hot ____.

8. My mom ____ a nurse last year.

9. These two pictures look the ____.

10. The ____ dog walked around on three legs.

Fun with Phonograms © 2000 Creative Teaching Press

A Handy Man

Dan was a very handy man. His plan was to turn junk into things people could use again. Whenever he saw some trash in a can, he put it into his tan van and brought it home. Once, he repaired the handle on an old frying pan. Another time, he fixed a broken fan so that it ran again. If you have something that you can't use anymore, give it to Dan. He can make it look brand-new again!

Can you find 13 different words with –an?

stand	handle	pan
fan	man	ran
planet	candle	van
		can

1. I _____ read and write very well.

2. Ask that _____ to help you lift up this box.

3. She _____ so fast she won the race.

4. Please help me put the cookies on the _____.

5. Turn on the _____ if you feel too hot.

6. Do you drive a car, a motorcycle, or a _____?

∗ 7. Will you _____ next to me?

∗ 8. Turn the _____ to open the door.

∗ 9. Let's light the _____ on the cake and sing "Happy Birthday."

∗ 10. Mars is the red _____.

Fun with Phonograms © 2000 Creative Teaching Press

Thank You

Remember when your best friend Hank

Told you your phone number when you drew a blank?

Even if you feel cranky one day,

You know he'll always ask you to play.

And, what do you say?

THANK YOU!

What if your favorite toy fell and sank

In your swanky, brand-new fish tank?

If your sister heard you shout,

You know she'd come to help you out.

And you would say without a doubt . . .

THANK YOU!

What if you and your brother Frank

Washed your jeans but then they shrank?

Just be honest and tell your dad.

I bet he laughs and doesn't get mad.

What would you say to show you're glad?

THANK YOU!

Can you find 9 different words with *-ank*?

Fun with Phonograms © 2000 Creative Teaching Press

Name _____   Date _____

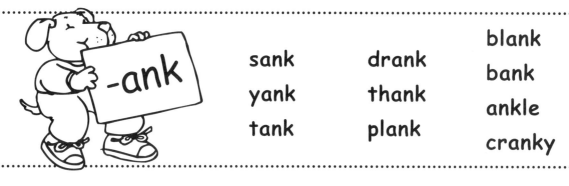

sank   drank   blank

yank   thank   bank

tank   plank   ankle

                           cranky

1. Don't _____ out your tooth. Let it fall out on its own.

2. My mom needs to go to the _____ to get some money.

3. She _____ all of her milk.

4. Write your name on the _____ line.

5. The ship _____ to the bottom of the sea.

6. He put some fish in the _____.

7. Remember to say "_____ you" when someone helps you.

8. There is a loose _____ on the dock.

* 9. I hurt my _____ when I tripped.

* 10. The boy woke up too early so he was _____.

After My Nap

After my nap, my dad asked me to wrap our sandwiches in some napkins. We were going on a hike through the woods. I put on my cap and got into the car. I kept a map on my lap in case we got lost on the way there. When we arrived, we looked for trees to tap for sap. We will use this sticky stuff to make syrup for our flapjacks. I saw a happy rabbit hop over a trap that a hunter had left. I heard a woodpecker rap on a tree with its beak. This is such a busy place. I think I need another nap!

Can you find 12 different words with –ap?

map   napkin   captain
tap   flap   happy
nap   cap   lap
                         sap

1. Can you swim a _____ in the pool?

2. Check the _____ if you get lost.

3. I wear a _____ on my head when I
   play baseball.

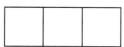

4. _____ on the door to see if she is home.

5. There is a lot of _____ in that tree.

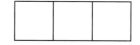

6. When I am tired, I like to take a _____.

7. Watch the flag _____ in the wind.

* 8. My teacher is always _____ to see us.

* 9. The _____ is in charge of
     the ship.

* 10. He needs a _____ to wipe his hands.

Fun with Phonograms © 2000 Creative Teaching Press

In a Flash

My mother handed me some cash.

She asked, "Can you make it to the store in a flash?

I need a sack of potatoes to mash."

"I'll dash right over on my super-charged bike.

I'll bring you anything you'd like.

That's why they call me Marvelous Mike."

As I ride to the store and back, I do not crash.

I don't want to have those potatoes smash.

I'm not in the mood for potato hash!

Can you find 7 different words with –ash?

lash	mash	trash
hash	sash	cash
dash	crash	stash
		flash

1. Wear a helmet in case you _____ on your bike.

2. Will you help me _____ these potatoes?

3. The red light will _____ when a train is coming.

4. Please throw the paper in the _____ can.

5. I need _____ to buy some food.

6. A _____ fell into my eye.

7. I will _____ my money in my piggy bank.

8. He will _____ over to the market to buy some bread.

9. Do you like to eat _____ browns for breakfast?

10. Ashley wore a red _____ on her dress.

Fun with Phonograms © 2000 Creative Teaching Press

Scat the Cat

I'm Scat, a magical cat.
I can change most anything—just like that!
I can change a baseball bat into a rat—
Thin or fat—just like that!

I can change a dog into a frog
Or into a log or even a hog.
I can make a ball go flat—
As flat as a mat—just like that!

I can turn a fan into a man
Who cooks his lunch in a frying pan.
I can turn a key into a bee
That lives in a hive in a tree.
Would you want to be just like me?

Can you find 8 different words with -at?

Fun with Phonograms © 2000 Creative Teaching Press

cat	pat	bat
shatter	mat	fat
flat	that	chat
		matter

1. Please wipe your feet on the _____.

2. The _____ purred softly.

3. Let's have a _____ over the phone.

4. We need a _____ and a ball to play baseball.

5. That ball will not bounce because it is too _____.

6. You deserve a _____ on the back.

7. The _____ on a bear helps keep it warm in the winter.

8. What is _____ noise?

* 9. You look sad. What is the _____?

* 10. The glass will _____ if you drop it.

Fun with Phonograms © 2000 Creative Teaching Press

Time to Celebrate

June 10th is the date of my brother Nate's birthday. We decided to celebrate by having a party. My sister Kate helped me decorate the house. All of our friends came, but John was a little late. He missed the first game but ate a plate of birthday cake with us later. Then Nate opened his presents. He got a new wheel for his skate, a pump to inflate his basketball, and a book about our state. Nate thanked all of his friends for the presents and us for a great birthday party.

Can you find 12 different words with –ate?

Fun with Phonograms © 2000 Creative Teaching Press

inflate	date	deflate
hate	late	plate
skate	mate	state
		gate

1. Try not to be _____ for school.

2. Did you remember to lock the _____?

3. Which is the biggest _____ in our country?

4. Please write the _____ on your paper.

5. We need to _____ the ball because it is flat.

6. I will _____ the beach ball so it will fit in my bag.

7. Where is the _____ to this sock?

8. I _____ scary movies.

9. I wear a helmet when I _____.

10. Would you like more beans on your _____?

Fun with Phonograms © 2000 Creative Teaching Press

The Lion's Paw

Once there was a lazy lion. It liked to crawl instead of run. One morning, the lion saw a little mouse run over its big paw. The lion loved raw meat, and the mouse would be a perfect meal. The lion was hungry, but it was also too lazy to chase after the mouse.

Every day, the mouse ran past the lion. One morning, the lion decided to lay down the law. It gently pinned the mouse to the ground with its claw. The mouse looked up and was afraid of the lion's big jaw. After a few minutes, the lion let the scared mouse go. The mouse learned a lesson—never tease a lion, even if it is lazy!

Can you find 7 different words with –aw?

Fun with Phonograms © 2000 Creative Teaching Press

law	caw	draw
thaw	paw	straw
crawl	raw	jaw
		saw

1. It is important to always obey the _____. □□□

2. Can you _____ a picture of an elephant? □□□□

3. This meat is still _____. □□□

4. I _____ you at the store yesterday. □□□

5. We will let this frozen pie _____ before we eat it. □□□□

6. My _____ is sore from chewing this gum. □□□

7. Don't get near a lion's _____! □□□

8. Would you like a _____ for your drink? □□□□□

9. The crow started to _____. □□□

* 10. Her baby sister just learned how to _____. □□□□

Fun with Phonograms © 2000 Creative Teaching Press

Do You Want to Play?

Do you want to play with me?

We can go and climb a tree.

Or we could play with some clay,

If your mom says that it's okay.

It doesn't matter what we do,

As long as I can stay with you.

We could pretend it's a holiday

And eat some cookies from a tray.

If you would rather sit and relax,

We could just play with some jacks.

Would you like to run a relay

Just like we did yesterday?

When it's time for you to go,

I'll be sad, but I will know . . .

You'll go away for only a day

And then we'll meet again—hooray!

Can you find 12 different words with -ay?

Fun with Phonograms © 2000 Creative Teaching Press

Name _____ Date _____

-ay

play   may   hay
clay   day   say
way   lay   stay
                  hooray

1. What _____ of the week is today?

2. Do you want to _____ a game with me?

3. I have to _____ home from school when I am sick.

4. I couldn't hear you. What did you _____?

5. The horse likes to eat _____.

6. Which _____ did he go?

7. I made a cat out of _____, and then I painted it.

8. The girl was so excited that she shouted, "_____!"

9. The dog wanted to _____ down to take a nap.

10. _____ I help you?

Fun with Phonograms © 2000 Creative Teaching Press

Treats to Eat

Would you like to eat cookies or cake?

Would you like to eat chicken or steak?

Would you like to eat fish or meat?

What is your favorite food to eat?

Have a tortilla—corn or wheat.

Try a strawberry—juicy and sweet.

Here's a brownie—what a treat!

Topped with ice cream—can't be beat!

It doesn't matter what you eat,

As long as you are very neat.

Come to the table and have a seat.

Can't you see it's time for a treat?

Can you find 7 different words with -eat?

beat	eat	treat
neat	cheat	meat
feat	wheat	heat
		seat

1. Do you like to eat _____ bread?

2. Find a _____ at the table.

3. Your writing is very _____.

4. I need to get out of the _____ and go into the shade.

5. My favorite _____ is ice cream.

6. A tiger likes to eat _____.

7. A good sport will play by the rules and never _____.

8. Where should we _____ our lunch?

9. We will try to _____ the other team.

10. Juggling is a hard _____.

A Bad Day for Nell

Today Nell had a bad day at school.

She was so sad and felt like a fool.

As soon as she heard the morning bell,

She knew that things would not go well.

It all started when the class sang a song—

"The Farmer in the Dell"—so Nell sang along.

Suddenly she tripped, and she fell.

And soon her ankle started to swell.

Next came the "We Can Spell!" game.

But the letters of *sell* she could not name.

When it was time to go home, Nell could not walk.

So her teacher called her mom, and they started to talk.

Nell's mom came, and teacher said, "Farewell!"

Then Nell went home and rested a spell.

Later, from her bed, Nell could smell a treat.

"Cookies!" she cried and jumped to her feet.

Nell was as good as new. Phew!

Can you find 10 different words with *-ell*?

Fun with Phonograms © 2000 Creative Teaching Press

fell	yell	shell
sell	spell	tell
bell	belly	yellow
		umbrella

1. Do you have anything to ____ at the garage sale?

2. Please do not ____ in the library.

3. I know how to ____ so many words!

4. Did you hear the school ____ ring?

5. Please ____ me a joke.

6. He ____ down and scraped his leg.

7. The turtle is safe in its ____.

* 8. A penguin likes to slide down the ice on its ____.

* 9. I carry an ____ when it rains.

*10. She wore a ____ dress.

Fun with Phonograms © 2000 Creative Teaching Press

How to Be the Best Guest

If you want to be the best, most polite guest,

Here are a few things that I would suggest.

Try not to bother another guest,

Or someone will think that you're a pest.

Treat others the way you want them to treat you,

And you may be invited back for a barbecue.

Never let your manners rest.

Who knows when they'll be put to the test!

Can you find 6 different words with -est?

best	west	chest
detest	rest	jester
pest	suggest	nest
		test

1. You did a great job if you tried your _____.

2. Who wants the _____ of the pizza?

3. Do you live on the east or _____ side of town?

4. How did you do on your math _____?

5. The gorilla was pounding on its _____.

6. How many eggs are in that _____?

7. Try not to bother others or they will think that you are a _____.

8. I _____ that you wear a jacket on this breezy day.

9. I _____ the smell of rotten eggs.

✳ 10. Have you ever watched a court _____ make people laugh?

Fun with Phonograms © 2000 Creative Teaching Press

Two Nice Mice

Two mice hid in their hole in the living room wall until everyone was asleep. Then they sneaked out and searched for leftover food. They found a slice of bread and some white rice that had fallen under the kitchen table. There was also a piece of popcorn with some kind of spice sprinkled on it. What a nice dinner! They were interrupted twice by the household cat, but they ran back out again both times in search of more food. They were careful to watch out for the mousetrap, a device that the people left on the floor to catch mice. Take their advice—always be careful and clever!

Can you find 8 different words with –ice?

Name _____   Date _____

-ice

twice   advice   spice
price   nice   vice
dice   mice   rice
                       slice

1. To play the game, roll the _____.

2. The _____ ate the cheese.

3. We can eat white or brown _____.

4. Who wants the last _____ of pizza?

5. I'll pay any _____ for that book.

6. I like the _____ that I taste on this chicken.

7. I've seen that movie _____, and I liked it both times!

8. I ask my dad for _____ when I have a problem.

9. My friends are very _____.

10. Biting my nails is my worst _____.

Fun with Phonograms © 2000 Creative Teaching Press

The Tricky Chick

Wow! Did you see that clever baby chicken? That slick fox saw the chick and began to lick its lips, so the tricky chick pretended to be sick. Luckily, the fox wasn't interested in eating a sick chick for dinner. The next time the chick wants to leave the henhouse, it should stick its head out and check to see if the fox is around. Otherwise, the chick will have to trick the fox again!

Can you find 8 different words with *-ick*?

thick	brick	trick
lick	chick	pick
quick	wick	stick
		sick

1. Did you see the yellow ____ at the farm?

2. I need to ____ my ice cream before it drips all over me.

3. My friend is not here because he is ____.

4. Watch my dog chase this ____.

5. Make it ____. I'm very late!

6. What color is the ____ on your house?

7. Which book did you ____ for your bedtime story?

8. That man showed me a card ____.

9. My dad lit the ____ on the candle.

10. The wool on a sheep is very ____.

Fun with Phonograms © 2000 Creative Teaching Press

Outside

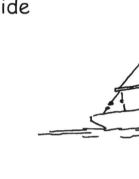

On a warm, sunny day,

Do you like to be outside

Where you can run

Or go down a slide?

Do you like to swim

And wade in the tide?

Or do you like to ride

Your bike over the hillside?

Sometimes it's so hard to decide

Whether you should stay inside

Or go outside to play with a friend

Until the warm weather comes to an end.

Whatever it is that we choose to do,

It must be fun for me and you.

We need to enjoy every day.

There are so many ways that we can play!

Can you find 7 different words with *-ide*?

Name _____ Date _____

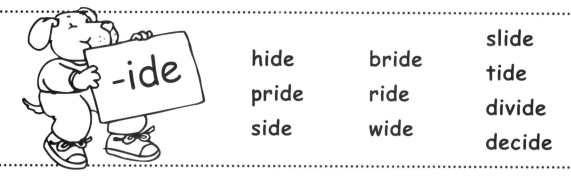

-ide

hide	bride	slide
pride	ride	tide
side	wide	divide
		decide

1. The _____ looked beautiful in her wedding gown.

2. Where did you _____ the extra key?

3. I went down the _____ at the park.

4. I can't _____ what I want to eat.

5. Let's _____ this cookie in half.

6. Do you know how to _____ a bike?

7. Always take _____ in your work.

8. Let's move over to the other _____ of the room.

9. This seat is not _____ enough for two people.

10. The _____ washed my sand castle away.

Fun with Phonograms © 2000 Creative Teaching Press

What a Fright!

In the middle of the night,
I woke up in fright.
I thought that I had seen a light
Shining in my window.

It gave me such an awful scare.
I could see nothing in the glare.
All I could do was sit and stare
Out of my window.

It wasn't lightning. It wasn't rain.
Neither was it my sister Jane.
My throat was tight. I was in pain.
What was outside my window?

I got a flashlight from under my bed.
I held it right up over my head.
I walked under the cover of my red bedspread
Over to my window.

I shined the light into the night,
And to my delight, there in my sight
Was a lovely full moon shining bright,
Reflecting off my window.

Can you find 10 different words with *-ight*?

-ight

height	might	flight
right	light	fight
tight	bright	night
		lightning

1. Do you draw with your left or your _____ hand?

2. What time do you go to bed at _____?

3. Please turn on the _____.

4. These shoes hurt my feet because they are too _____.

5. The news reported that it _____ rain tomorrow.

6. The sun is so _____ that I need my sunglasses.

7. We took a long _____ on an airplane.

8. I wonder if I will grow to the same _____ as my brother.

9. Don't _____ with your sister.

*10. Thunder follows _____ in a storm.

Fun with Phonograms © 2000 Creative Teaching Press

Over the Hill with Jack and Jill

Over where the water runs still,

There is a well upon a hill.

Jack and Jill ran to the well.

But on the way back they tripped and fell.

Upon the hill the water did spill.

And once again there was a pail to fill.

"We will give it one more try!"

And they got water by and by.

Can you find 6 different words with *-ill*?

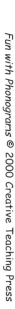
Fun with Phonograms © 2000 Creative Teaching Press

chill	will	pill
fill	spill	bill
mill	hill	gill
		still

1. How much is the _____ for our lunch?

2. There is a _____ in the air tonight.

3. Fish have a _____ on either side of their head.

4. Try not to _____ that red punch on the carpet.

5. I _____ help you soon.

6. Please stand _____ for the picture.

7. The doctor gave me a _____ for my sore throat.

8. It is hard to ride your bike up a _____.

9. Will you please _____ up the car with gas?

10. The hen took the wheat to the _____.

66

Fun with Phonograms © 2000 Creative Teaching Press

The Twins

Meet two twin brothers named Lin and Fin.

Each has a dimple on his chin.

They always do things to make their friends grin.

One silly day, Fin yelled, "Ready, set, begin!"

And both of the brothers started to spin.

What a silly contest—who will win?

Their only prize will be a bruise on each shin!

Can you find 10 different words with *-in?*

win	thin	fin
spin	tin	pin
shin	skin	begin
		twin

1. My hair is too _____ to braid.

2. That dolphin slapped the water with its _____.

3. It doesn't matter if you _____ or lose.

4. That boy looks just like you. Is he your _____?

5. This rash on my _____ itches.

6. At what time does your school _____?

7. I like to _____ around in circles.

8. I'll use a safety _____ to attach my name tag.

9. That can is made out of _____.

10. I fell down and scraped my _____.

Fun with Phonograms © 2000 Creative Teaching Press

In the Sunshine

A cat walked in the bright sunshine
With eight of its feline friends.
They proudly walked in a very straight line
Down to where the river ends.

They were hungry cats and wanted to dine,
So they searched for a very fine lunch.
Then they saw plenty of food for all nine—
A river full of fish to munch!

Can you find 6 different words with *-ine*?

-ine

line	mine	fine
vine	nine	dine
pine	whine	shine
		combine

1. When you go out to eat, where do you like to _____?

2. Can you see that big _____ tree?

3. Please don't _____ when you don't get what you want.

4. My favorite number is _____.

5. My library book was late, so I had to pay a _____.

6. That jacket is not _____.

7. Please wait in _____ quietly.

8. We can _____ our money to buy that game.

9. The sun will _____ all day.

10. Grapes grow on a _____.

Fun with Phonograms © 2000 Creative Teaching Press

Anything for Me?

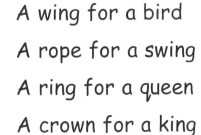

A wing for a bird
A rope for a swing
A ring for a queen
A crown for a king

A ping for a pong
A sting for a bee
A ding for a dong
Anything for me?

Can you find 8 different words with *-ing*?

-ing

sing   thing   sting

string   wing   swing

sling   ring   spring

                    bring

1. You don't want to bother that bee or it may _____ you.

2. Look at that pretty _____ on her finger!

3. What did you _____ for a snack today?

4. The flowers bloom in the _____.

5. That ladybug has two dots on each _____.

6. What is that _____ over there?

7. Do you like to _____ songs?

8. The _____ on my kite snapped.

9. I broke my arm, so I have to wear a _____.

10. An ape can _____ on a vine.

Fun with Phonograms © 2000 Creative Teaching Press

A Pink Drink at the Rink

"Let's go to the ice rink," said Eric. "I think that's a great idea!" said Zachary. They went to the rink and skated for a while. Then they decided to find a snack. They each bought a pink drink and some popcorn to share. Eric sprinkled some salt on the popcorn before they ate it. Then Zachary said, "What is that smell? It stinks! I think the hot dogs are burning." The smoke made the boys blink. Eric said, "Let's pass on the hot dogs today!" and they both laughed.

Can you find 7 different words with -ink?

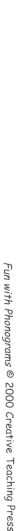

think	sink	blink
link	pink	stink
rink	wink	drink
		mink

1. Do you like the color _____?

2. Please wash the dishes in the _____.

3. Do you _____ your eyes when it is windy?

4. I went to the skating _____.

5. Did you just _____ your eye at me?

6. What is that smell? Does it _____!

7. What do you _____ will happen in the next chapter of our book?

8. I could use a _____ of lemonade on this hot day!

9. She does not have a _____ coat.

10. Let's _____ arms and skate together.

Fun with Phonograms © 2000 Creative Teaching Press

Before My Trip

"Snip!" went the scissors. "Zip!" went the razor. One more clip, and my hair was finally ready. I gave the barber a tip and walked out the door. I had some time before my ship was to sail, so I stopped for lunch. As I was eating, I thought about my trip. I was going to spend a week on an island. I couldn't wait to walk on the sand and take a dip in the sea. I took one more sip of my drink and ate my last chip. Then I went to the slip where my boat was waiting. I was off to sea at last!

Can you find 10 different words with *-ip*?

Name _____   Date _____

-ip

flip	rip	hip
chip	sip	drip
dip	lip	tip
		trip

1. Where did you go on your _____?

2. My drink is so hot that I can only _____ it.

3. One more potato _____, and then I'm full.

4. I can help my dad _____ the pancakes.

5. Did you remember to leave a _____ for our waitress?

6. A mother can carry her baby on her _____.

7. I put some _____ on my crackers.

8. Try not to _____ the paper.

9. There is a slow _____ coming from the sink.

10. I fell and bit my _____.

Fun with Phonograms © 2000 Creative Teaching Press

The Fir

"Kind Sir, please tell me what this tree might be."

"Why, it's a fir, my friend. Can't you see?"

The beauty of it caused my heart to stir.

So tall, so green, so mighty—this fir!

Can you find 3 different words with -ir?

-ir

dirt	shirt	third
stir	bird	sir
first	fir	thirsty
		thirteen

1. Thank you, _____, for your advice.

2. Do you want to help me _____ the brownie mix?

3. Pinecones grow on _____ trees.

* 4. The boy blew out three candles on his _____ birthday.

* 5. Your pants match your _____ nicely.

* 6. I like to be the _____ in line.

* 7. An eagle is a very big _____.

* 8. I get _____ after I run.

* 9. Some people think that the number _____ is unlucky.

* 10. My baby sister likes to play in the _____.

Fun with Phonograms © 2000 Creative Teaching Press

Guess What's in My Pocket

Try to guess what's in my pocket.

Is it a rocket or is it a locket?

I'll give you just a clue or two,

So you can guess what I'm hiding from you.

This thing is small and you use it every day.

It can chime or ring or even say,

"Ticktock, ticktock, tick-tock-tock."

What's in my pocket? Yes, it's a clock!

This thing always comes in a pair.

And it's something soft to wear.

Wear it on a carpet and you might get a shock.

What's in my pocket? Yes, it's a sock!

You need this thing to keep others out

And to keep your things safe without a doubt.

Open it with a key—not a block.

What's in my pocket? Yes, it's a lock!

Can you find 9 different words with -ock?

flock	frock	knock
pocket	lock	clock
dock	smock	sock
		shock

1. Did you hear a _____ at the door?

2. Please _____ the door when you leave.

3. Does it _____ you that I don't like ice cream?

4. I will wait on the _____ for the boat.

5. Can you read the time on the _____?

6. A group of sheep is called a _____.

7. A dress can also be called a _____.

8. I wear a _____ when I paint.

9. My toe sticks out of the hole in my _____.

* 10. I carry my money in my _____.

Fun with Phonograms © 2000 Creative Teaching Press

These Riddles Are No Joke

It is a vegetable.

It is green.

You take it apart to eat it.

What is it?

(An artichoke)

It is something you say.

It makes people laugh.

It is funny.

What is it?

(A joke)

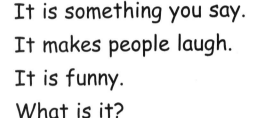

This is something you do with your arms.

You can do this on your front or your back.

You use this to swim in the water.

(A stroke)

It is gray.

It floats through the air like a cloud.

It tells you that a fire is about to start.

(Smoke)

Can you find 4 different words with *-oke*?

Name _____ Date _____

-oke

token	stroke	smoke
poke	woke	awoke
broke	spoke	choke
		joke

1. When the frame fell on the floor, it _____.

2. She _____ very quietly in the library.

3. Please do not _____ me with your pencil.

4. Try to eat small bites so that you will not _____on your food.

5. I _____ up early today.

6. My friend told me a funny _____.

7. The fire made a lot of _____.

8. My dog likes me to _____ its back.

9. I _____ to the sound of singing birds.

* 10. May I borrow a _____ to play this game?

Fun with Phonograms © 2000 Creative Teaching Press

82

The Hopping Bunny

Ann watched the bunny's ears flop every time it went hopping through the garden. The bunny stopped to munch on a carrot top. Even though Ann was there, it did not stop eating. Ann was eating, too. She was busy drinking a can of pop she bought at the shop on the corner. Ann decided that before she came to the garden the next time, she would chop some cabbage for this funny bunny. Then Ann saw the bunny drop the stem of the carrot and scamper away.

Can you find 9 different words with –op?

Name _____   Date _____

-op

top	pop	crop
shop	slop	hop
mop	stop	chop
		lollipop

1. The bunny likes to _____ through the garden.

2. We need to _____ the floor.

3. _____ when the light turns red.

4. Where do you _____ for shoes?

5. Will you help me _____ the vegetables for our soup?

6. I try my best, so my work will not look like _____.

7. Please don't _____ my balloon.

8. I brought a _____ for you to eat.

9. Let's race to the _____ of the hill.

10. The farmer planted a _____ of beans.

Fun with Phonograms © 2000 Creative Teaching Press

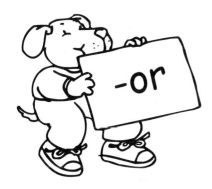

A Letter from Salvador

Fun with Phonograms © 2000 Creative Teaching Press

Dear Señor,

Thank you for taking me on a tour of Mexico. I had never seen a condor sitting in its nest nor a matador fight a big, strong bull before. Next time, can we look for lizards or dive for seashells?

Sincerely,

Salvador

Can you find 8 different words with *-or*?

-or

forget	popcorn	for
horn	cord	story
sport	born	short
		horse

1. I know what to get you ____ your birthday.

* 2. Tennis is my favorite ____.

* 3. Would you like to ride on a ____?

* 4. In what month were you ____?

* 5. He is too ____ to reach the top shelf.

* 6. I will play the ____ in our band.

* 7. I tied a ____ around the package.

* 8. I like to eat ____ when I watch a movie.

* 9. Did you ____ to lock the door?

* 10. I wrote a ____ about a frog and a duck.

Fun with Phonograms © 2000 Creative Teaching Press

Snore Some More

One night, I couldn't fall asleep because I could hear my dad snore all the way in my room. I tried to ignore it, but I couldn't. He began to snore some more. When this happened once before, I went into his room and woke him up. I didn't think he would want an encore of that night, so I left him alone. I adore my dad, and I don't want him to be sore at me. Tomorrow I think I will go to the store to buy some earplugs.

Can you find 8 different words with –ore?

Fun with Phonograms © 2000 Creative Teaching Press

Name _____ Date _____

-ore

store	adore	score
more	tore	wore
snore	chore	sore
		before

1. Do you _____ when you sleep?

2. What is the _____ of the game?

3. My main _____ is to wash the dishes.

4. Would you like some _____ cookies?

5. Let's read a story _____ we go to sleep.

6. He will buy some milk and eggs at the _____.

7. I have a _____ on my knee.

8. She _____ the newspaper in half.

9. I _____ my baby sister because she is so cute!

10. I like that hat you _____ yesterday.

Fun with Phonograms © 2000 Creative Teaching Press

In the Muck

Look at what we found stuck in this muck.

There is a shoe, a shovel, and a hockey puck.

We'll put it all in the back of our truck

And sell it in town for maybe a buck.

Now the pond will be ready for you, little duck.

And you can live happily with any luck!

Can you find 7 different words with *-uck*?

duck	stuck	tuck
suck	truck	bucket
luck	cluck	mucky
		buckle

1. I like to ride in my grandpa's _____.

2. The car got _____ in the mud.

3. My mom wished me good _____ as I left for my soccer game.

4. The white _____ swam through the pond.

5. I like it when my parents _____ me in at night.

6. I do not _____ my thumb anymore.

7. "_____!" said the hen.

* 8. I don't want to swim in _____ water.

* 9. Do you want to fill the _____ with sand?

* 10. I help my sister _____ her seat belt.

Fun with Phonograms © 2000 Creative Teaching Press

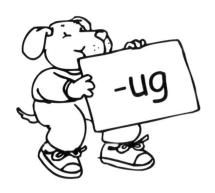

Bugs

Have you ever dug deep in the dirt

For a bug to keep in the pocket of your shirt?

Have you ever tried to pick up a slippery slug

Or catch the roly-poly that lives under your rug?

Have you ever tried to catch a waterbug

To keep as a pet in a coffee mug?

If you do not want to try any of these things,

Then look up, not down, for some bugs with wings.

Can you find 6 different words with *-ug*?

-ug

snug   plug   bug
dug   tug   lug
hug   mug   juggle
                rug

1. The spider caught a _____ in its web.

2. I want to give you a _____.

3. My teacher drinks tea out of a _____.

4. Did she just spill her soup on the _____?

5. I feel warm and _____ in my bed.

6. Please don't _____ on my jacket.

7. He _____ a hole deep in the dirt.

8. Be careful when you _____ in a lamp.

9. I have to _____ this heavy backpack home from school.

* 10. Do you know how to _____ three balls?

Fun with Phonograms © 2000 Creative Teaching Press

Thump, Bump, Clump, Jump

Thump, thump, thump
Went the hippo, oh, so plump.

Bump, bump, bump
Went the rhino and its rump.

Clump, clump, clump
Went the camel with its hump.

Jump, jump, jump
Went the horse over the stump!

Can you find 8 different words with *-ump*?

Name _____   Date _____

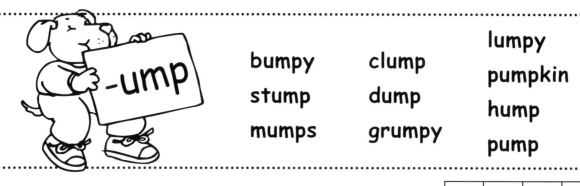

bumpy   clump   lumpy
stump   dump   pumpkin
mumps   grumpy   hump
                   pump

1. The camel has a _____ on its back.

2. I sat on a tree _____ in the park.

3. The trash goes to the _____.

4. He threw a big _____ of snow at me.

5. She helped him _____ the water out
   of the well.

* 6. He woke up too early so he was
     a bit _____.

* 7. The road was very _____.

* 8. When I was sick with the _____,
     I stayed in bed for days.

* 9. My oatmeal is _____.

* 10. We eat _____ pie on
      Thanksgiving Day.

Fun with Phonograms © 2000 Creative Teaching Press

The Treasure That Sunk

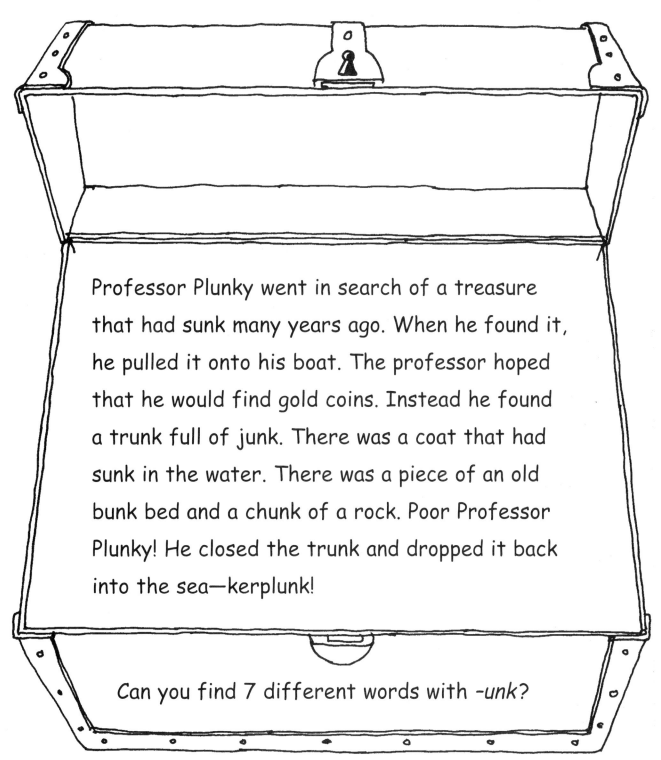

Professor Plunky went in search of a treasure that had sunk many years ago. When he found it, he pulled it onto his boat. The professor hoped that he would find gold coins. Instead he found a trunk full of junk. There was a coat that had sunk in the water. There was a piece of an old bunk bed and a chunk of a rock. Poor Professor Plunky! He closed the trunk and dropped it back into the sea—kerplunk!

Can you find 7 different words with -unk?

-unk

bunk	chunky	dunk
hunk	spunk	sunk
junk	shrunk	trunk
		skunk

1. My keys have _____ to the bottom of the lake.

2. I try not to eat too much _____ food.

3. She got her jacket out of the _____ of her car.

4. I like to sleep on the top _____.

5. A _____ has a white stripe on its tail.

6. Do you like to _____ your cookies into milk?

7. My friend has a lot of energy. She is full of _____!

8. My blue sweater has _____ in the wash.

9. I ate a _____ of cheese for a snack.

* 10. I like my peanut butter to be _____ with lots of nuts.

Fun with Phonograms © 2000 Creative Teaching Press